TWENTY CURATED BUSINESS IDEAS

Volume 1

by

Jack Lookman

Copyright © 2022 Jack Lookman Limited

All rights reserved.

No portion of this book may be reproduced in whole or in part, in any form or by any means, electronic or mechanical including photocopying, recording, or by any information storage and retrieval system, without the consent and written permission from the author.

INTRODUCTION

This work is A Collection Of 20 Curated Business Ideas By Jack Lookman; presented in simple and easy-to-comprehend English.

Some of them come in poetic expressions, and could be entertaining.

The aim is to trigger the thought processes of readers, such that they could either explore the ideas, or the presented ideas could stimulate others.

This is a collection of 20 thoughts, and we intended to create further volumes.

We aim to make the collection available in audio and text formats on our different platforms.

The content is also available in physical and digital formats.

It's hoped, that it could add value to society and help in creating business and employment opportunities.

It's also hoped, that they shall create economically vibrant societies.

Have a great read.

Ire lotun, ire losi, ire lopolopo (I wish you lots of blessings from all directions)

Olayinka Carew aka Jack Lookman

© Jack Lookman Limited 2022

jacklookman@yahoo.co.uk

ACKNOWLEDGEMENT

The foundational sacrifices of my parents are much appreciated; they invested in giving me a good education.

This was within and outside the classroom.

Contributions of Mr Sunday Rotimi DAVIS-OLUBAYO, are much appreciated.

The indirect support of others is also appreciated.

Thank you very much to one and all.

Olayinka Carew aka Jack Lookman.

https://www.jaaloo.com
https://jacklookman.co.uk
https://www.jacksempowerment.com

DEDICATION

This piece of work is dedicated to all my family members.

My Late Dad

My Mum

My Siblings

My Children

May Allah grant us the best of this world and the hereafter and protect us from the torment of hell fire, torment of the grave, and all other torments.

Ameen.

At Jack Lookman Limited, Our mission is to Empower and Inspire Generations by leveraging the Internet

LIST OF ARTICLES

1. CONTENT CREATION

2. CATARRH REPUBLIC

3. BLOGGING WITHOUT MONEY

4. MONETISING ONLINE TERMS AND CONDITIONS

5. TELECOMMUNICATIONS

6. CROWD LEVERAGE

7. YORUBA ISLAMIC QUESTIONS AND ANSWERS

8. GETTING THE BEST OF VOLUNTEERS AND STAFF

9. I WANT TO START A BUSINESS BUT HAVE NO MONEY

10. PERSONAL SAFETY GADGETS

11. HALAL BUSINESS MICRO FINANCE

12. YORUBA PROJECT

13. FREELANCE BRAINSTORMING

14. BATH SPONGE

15. LEVERAGING RELIGIOUS ORGANISATIONS

16. LISTING WEBSITES FOR NIGERIANS IN DIASPORA

17. EMPOWERING YOUNG GRADUATES IN NIGERIA

18. X BUSINESSES YOU COULD START FOR Y THOUSAND NAIRA

19. GROOMING VOLUNTEERS, INTERNS AND JOB SEEKERS

20. MONETISING FAMILY UNIONS

●1. CONTENT CREATION

The words content creation could be intimidating for some.

Some feel it's very intellectual;

Needing to have loads of knowledge and authority.

They could partly be true;

But you could start the journey

And then build on it as you go along.

You need to choose a niche

And create content around it.

You could do it individually,

You could collaborate or have a team

It's suggested to leverage a niche of interest.

And one whose usage could pay the bills

Look for a subject area that interests you;

Research it and carry out due diligence.

Ensure that you could profit from it

Otherwise the efforts be unsustainable

Research your competitors;

The market place; etc.

Your content could be in one or more formats.

It could be text, audio or video.

The text could be on platforms such as ebooks, paperbacks, blogs, etc.
While the audio or video could be on different platforms

Social media, blogs, youtube, facebook, podcast, etc.

You could upload the same content to multiple platforms.
And by the way, some of these platforms are free to use;

But you'd need to do marketing, etc to attract the crowd.

The content needs to be of great value, engaging and very well presented.

We shall share some case studies of content ideas in later editions.

It's hoped that this shall stimulate your thought process;
As well as inspire you to greater actions

As you share great value with your audience;
The audience is likely to grow.

As the audience grows;
The chances of monetisation are higher.

If you require mentoring on this, please feel free to contact me.

You could also educate yourself via content on the internet; or via books.

You could do content creation as a side or main hustle.

Apart from monetary gains;

More importantly is the impact that you'd create

Not only for your immediate audience

But for generations untold.

In some cases, to optimise your value proposition

You may need to invest money and resources

If this is a challenge, you could:

- Collaborate

- Seek Investors

Or Crowdfund

Feel free to contact me for more in-depth thoughts.

Feel free to book mentoring at Jack The Mentor via https://www.jacksempowerment.com

Some basic requirements to start, are:

- Content (what you wish to share with your audience)

- A platform or platforms (Social media, blog, etc)

- A digital device or devices (tablet, laptop or desktop)

- A podcast channel (as necessary) (for audio content)

- An Amazon account (for ebooks and paperbacks)

- Determination

- A Team (as necessary)

- A mentor (as necessary)

- Research skills

- Internet access

- A Youtube channel (as necessary)

- A Facebook account (as necessary)

- Google Adsense Account (for monetising some platforms) (as necessary)

- A Marketing strategy (to effectively reach your desired audience)

Some tools that you could employ, are:

- search engine optimisation tools

- keyword research tools

- content idea generating tools

- etc

I hope that you found value.

Please share your thoughts; and share this content with those whom it may benefit.

A Collection Of Curated Business Ideas By Jack Lookman

2. CATARRH REPUBLIC

During some climatic seasons such as summer and winter;

People suffer from sneezing, coughing, hay fever etc.

Some of them use handkerchiefs and some use disposable tissues.

While some others use water to clean the mucus and dirt.

The problem is that; especially for those who use these options; they could very easily spread germs.

This applies to children, youths and adults. And probably globally.

Some of the children will spread the germs to their eyes, thus making the eyes irritable.

Some don't effectively dispose of the the tissues or handkerchiefs.

They could keep them in their handbags or in pockets of clothes etc.

Either way, germs are still spread.

Though there may be different solutions to the problem, they may not work for everyone.

The proposed solution is the creation and marketing of purpose made small bags.

You could decide on the material of choice, and these could be disposable or reusable.

The bags could be opened or sealed via a string. You open it by puling-open the top; and seal it by pulling the string.

The use of tissues and/ or handkerchiefs could still continue anyway.

The bag could however be used for disposal or recycling.

In addition to this, a spray or disinfectant, could be a complimentary product.

The recent effects of the Corona Virus epidemic could add to the urgency of creating these products.

The production line could start with the production of the bags. You could prioritise the disposable or reusable ones. And then proceed to the next.

Tissues and handkerchiefs could be sourced and sold as well; so is the disinfectant.

Online stores could be created, with different distribution channels or networks.

Benefits of these product/s include:

* job creation

*wealth creation

*improved hygiene

*improved health

*improved well-being

etc.

Though this business could be capital intensive, there are opportunities for various value chains.

The products are relevant globally, and the business model could also be franchised.

Please contact me to discuss details, if interested.

A Collection Of Curated Business Ideas By Jack Lookman

3. BLOGGING WITHOUT MONEY

Creating a blog without money.

I wish to create a blog;

But I have no money.

I'm a university graduate without a job.

I'm motivated and knowledgeable.

I love to learn and share

But have limitations

As well as constraints.

With each stride I take;

I face lots of obstacles.

I'm hungry for success;

And time is ticking and going.

I see great potential in creating a blog.

But don't have finance.

I could share knowledge;

Lots of experience and all.

I could benefit society and monetise.

But my challenge is money.

I need money to buy a domain.

I need to buy hosting

I need to have a computer.

I also need internet.

Oooh there are obstacles.

May be I could collaborate with others;

We could have a profit sharing formula.

May be we could have an agreement;

So that conflict could be eliminated.

May be I could lessen the load;

By delegating to suitable others.

May be I could include a financier;

This could be a classmate or friend.

May be I could do a business plan;

This could guide the journey we tread.

May be we could manage risks;

To reduce any liabilities.

May be we could articulate work streams;

So that we all know what to do.

May be we could have an exit strategy;

For those who wish to move on.

May be we could have a marketing plan;

So that customers know about us.

May be we could sort out legalities;

That we may not get into trouble.

May be we could do our budgeting;

To ensure we are not in the red.

May be we could brainstorm regularly;

And carry out research too.

May be we could leverage our strengths;

This is the power of team work.

May be we could have our plans;

Project, marketing and business.

May be we could start as small;

And grow an empire.

May be we should have a team;

With those of positive minds.

May be we should be transparent and accountable;

So that way we could build trust.

May be we should take that first step;

It's the beginning of a thousand miles.

<u>A Collection Of Curated Business Ideas By Jack Lookman</u>

4. MONETISING ONLINE TERMS AND CONDITIONS

I notice some big brands

On the internet and all

They have terms and conditions

That may take a life time to read

They also have them in very small prints

And then update them frequently

You need to agree to use the product

Or may not proceed at all

If you decide to call

It may take ages and dollars

Only to be told

That you have no choice

If you use the internet

And make purchases too

This story of mine

May be very familiar

But the point I'm making

Is the entrepreneurial opportunity

Bringing to mind,

Points to bear

You may decide to have a Youtube channel

With 'some points to note'

And summarise the small print

In simple audio

It may contain text

Or better 'audio'

In simple language

As well as with time stamps

Because of the changes

By the companies

You'd always be profitable

And make money

You'd include dates

And also choose your niche

Your target audience

Are online purchasers

Whats the problem you're solving

This you may ask

But think about the devil

In the little print

That may hunt you sooner

Or even later

You may ask if

Anyone reads the small print

You may carry out a survey

If you wish to know

You may ask if this will benefit any

Or they're happy to spend

But the pain that could be inflicted

Would answer such

With the hustle and bustle

And rat race too

The short attention span

And little cash too

May be a Youtube channel could do the job

Save money, time and effort too

This may save peace of mind

After all the grammar

You may ask what's product?

Its a Youtube channel

Notifying buyers of

Points to note

Points to note in terms and conditions

You shall include a disclaimer too

This shall protect, from litigation

This shall be for major players on the internet.

To protect the interest

Of you and me

A Collection Of Curated Business Ideas By Jack Lookman

5. TELECOMMUNICATIONS

Have you tried contacting people over the phone?...

By whatsapp, calling apps, etc?

Especially those in developing countries?

What's been your user experience?

Did the call go smoothly?

Were there network issues ?

Was the experience poor ?

Does this happen once?

Or does it happen regularly?

Are your calls for domestic,...

Or for business reasons?

Is the call experience very frustrating?

Do you spend time lamenting and complaining?

Or do you see a business opportunity?

Could you find a solution to the problem?

Could you design a solution?

Could you employ an engineer to design a solution?

Could you outsource the solution?...

The design, the manufacturing, the production, etc?

Could you research the market place?...
Nationally and globally?

Is there already a solution?

If so, could you adapt it to your needs?

Could you market it?

Could you be an Affiliate Marketer?

Could you monetise?

Could you explore the value chain?...
And plug in yourself where you fit?

Could this be a business opportunity?...
Especially in these days of unemployment?

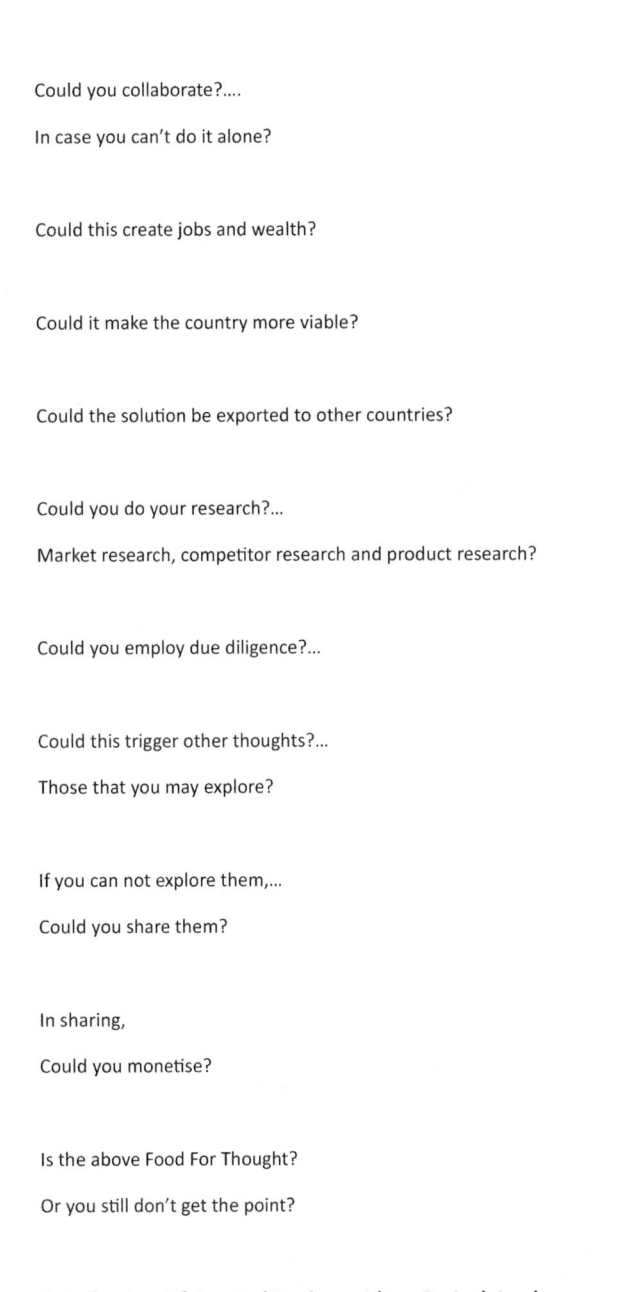

Could you collaborate?....

In case you can't do it alone?

Could this create jobs and wealth?

Could it make the country more viable?

Could the solution be exported to other countries?

Could you do your research?...

Market research, competitor research and product research?

Could you employ due diligence?...

Could this trigger other thoughts?...

Those that you may explore?

If you can not explore them,...

Could you share them?

In sharing,

Could you monetise?

Is the above Food For Thought?

Or you still don't get the point?

A Collection Of Curated Business Ideas By Jack Lookman

6. CROWD LEVERAGE

Have you noticed that some people have very good ideas

But these get buried in the grave

This could be for a variety of reasons...

Lack of finance

Lack of the right team

Lack of mentoring

Lack of drive or motivation

etc.

Their primary asset may be just the idea.

In the digital world we are

This has opened opportunities that could be explored

You could easily get:

The research outsourced

You could get franchisors

You could get marketers

You could get mentors

You could get investors;

etc.

You may perfect your idea

And carry out due diligence

You could collaborate

With necessary others

You could have an agreement

And a Profit Sharing Formula

You could leverage each other

To attain a common goal

You could leverage your network

Your colleagues and classmates

Those you've known

Recently and historically

You could leverage similar minds

Known individually or through the internet

You could articulate your thoughts and plans

And keep updating them

———————————————————————————————

Networking may also be good

As your network is your net-worth

Have a legally binding document

To protect all interests

Carry out due diligence

As all that glitter is not gold

Do relevant research on the market

And also of competitors

Explore the various opportunities

That the project may bring

Brainstorm as necessary

Individually and collectively

Articulate the business plan

And other relevant plans

Dot every i and cross every t

Start small

And grow very big

Market yourself and your idea

Leverage Social media, etc.

Articulate the relevant work streams,

And get ready when opportunity knocks

These are some thoughts

To profit the ideas

A Collection Of Curated Business Ideas By Jack Lookman

7. YORUBA ISLAMIC QUESTIONS AND ANSWERS

Islam is probably very misunderstood

By some Muslims and non Muslims

As a result of this

Misinformation floods the air

Also some Muslims recite prayers in Arabic

Without knowing the meanings

Or being conscious of such

Some of the Quranic writings are prayers

While some are curses

But some Muslims will say Amen

Without understanding or consciousness

We are told that Islam is a religion of knowledge

And not just common sense

You need to seek knowledge

To have a greater understanding

I am also aware that we live in a rat race

Where most people are chasing money and survival

They have short attention spans

And may not be bothered to spend hours

To research or to learn

I'm also aware of what's called technology

Internet, smart phone, Social media, etc

These could be leveraged

To pass the message

When I require short and sharp answers

To an Islamic issue

I go to Youtube

To find an answer

Some of the responses may be 1-9 minutes long

Which could easily suit the purpose of the rat chasers

Short, sharp and to the point

Very concise answers

But there are audiences

That may not speak English

They may be Yorubas

Or speakers of other languages

———————————————————————————————————

Could the Youtube model above be replicated?...

For the speakers of Yoruba...

And for other languages?

Could there be concise answers...

To common and uncommon questions?

Could there be a replication of the English Youtube channels?

Could it benefit Yoruba Muslims?

Could it benefit other ethnicities?

Could it help the spread of Islam?

Could it help the understanding of Islam?

Could it inspire Yoruba Muslims and non Muslims

Who want to learn more?

Could it trigger the appetite for learning?

Could it help the world become a better place?

Could it help attract non Muslims to the deen?

Could it add value to one and all?

Could it be sadaqah jariyah?

Could you monetise the process?

Could you publish this on multiple platforms?...
Youtube, Facebook, podcast, etc?

If you don't need the money...
Could you donate to charity?

Do you get my point?

Could there be benefits for one and all?

Could it be a win-win?

Is there a need to carry out due diligence?...
To research, consult and pray istikharah?

Do you need to analyse the SWOT?...
Strengths, weaknesses, opportunities and threats?

Do you get my point?

———————————————————————————————

Creating audio or video content...

Explaining Islam...

In short, sharp and concise answers...

In Yoruba language or other languages of choice?

———————————————————————————————

Some basic resources required are:

-understanding of Yoruba language (or language of choice)

-a platform for the dissemination; eg; Youtube channel, Facebook, podcast, etc

-knowledge of Islam

-basic technical skills for uploads

-basic video editing skills

-digital devices e.g; smart phones, tablets or computers

-wisdom

-collaborators (as necessary)

-bank account (of your choice to monetise)

-etc

A Collection Of Curated Business Ideas By Jack Lookman

8. GETTING THE BEST OF VOLUNTEERS AND STAFF

Voluntary Organisations, Non Governmental Organisations

And Charity Organisations

Generally use volunteers

Some, if not most of the volunteers, are not formally trained

This may be due to financial constraints

Or because there are no proper systems and structures in place

Yet the output from volunteers

Could be multiplied;

And resources effectively managed

Time and effort may be effectively used

And the stress and strain on all parties minimised

All it takes is an investment in training

This may be once or in instalments

The training could contain specific and generic content

Membership sites could be leveraged for suitable access.

Audio, video and text could be used

The content could come from 'experts'

Internally, externally or both

Volunteers and staff could have access as necessary

The access could be paid- for, by the organisation

Individuals or by sponsors

Although there may be cost implications

The return on investment could be multiplied

Apart from adding value to the organisation

It also adds value to the individuals, community and society

You may ask how this is a business idea

As a Content Creator

You could create and articulate the content

You could either be the custodian...

Or you sell or manage it;

Terms and condition will apply

You could replicate this business model to different organisations

And make money by so doing

Some skills required for the business, are:

-basic information technology skills

-basic video editing skills

-negotiation skills

-communication skills

-inter-personal skills

-Research and Development skills

-networking skills

-marketing skills

If you don't have the skills

You could partner or collaborate with third parties

In order to compliment yours

Some resources required, are:

-digital devices -e.g tablet or computer

-access to the internet

-human resource (as necessary)

Benefits:

-It saves training time

-It's easily accessible (anywhere and anytime)

-Training costs are reduced

-It's effective

-It could be updated as necessary

-It's cost effective

-it's flexible

-It adds value to the organisation, staff and volunteers

-It adds value to the society

A Collection Of Curated Business Ideas By Jack Lookman

9. I WANT TO START A BUSINESS BUT HAVE NO MONEY

You may have the intellect

And you may have the drive

You may have the inspiration and vision

To start a business

You may have the idea

One which could change the world

You may have it in your head

Ready to download

But you have no money

To execute and monetise

You haven't all the resources

To convert the dream to reality

You are passionate about it

You see great value

But very few appreciate your gift

The value proposition offered

Could you articulate your thoughts...?

Dotting the i's and crossing the t's?

Could you do research...

Market, competitors and product?

Could you perfect your idea...

Incase opportunity knocks?

Could you invest in networking...

May be you could meet collaborators?

Could you research the internet...

For collaborators and investors?

Could you explore crowdfunding...

For investment and constructive criticism?

Could you leverage your network...

Is the network the net worth?

Could money be one part of resource...?

There may be other ingredients too

Could you explore the value chain...?

Just as I'm doing?

Would you let your dream and vision die...

Just because you lack money?

The answer is definitely blowing...

Right there in the wind.

A Collection Of Curated Business Ideas By Jack Lookman

10. PERSONAL SAFETY GADGETS

Some of us may be aware of reported insecurity

In Nigeria and some other countries

People get kidnapped

And released at the parting of cash

In some cases, when the ransom is paid

The asking gets escalated

In some cases, lives are lost

Creating lots of heartache

This issue affects local people

As well as travellers

It is gold mine for kidnappers

As sad as may be

Lets take a critical look

Through entrepreneurial eyes

This presents a business opportunity

That may bring hope

Could personal safety gadgets be helpful?

Could there be a variety of such gadgets?

Could there be a value chain...?

Involving different players?

Could Engineers play a part?

Could marketers play a part?

Could designers play a part?

Could salesmen do?...

Could distributors do?

Could there be a place for product finders?

Could the gadgets be manufactured in Nigeria?

Could they be sourced from else where?

Could job opportunity be created?

Could wealth opportunity be created?

Could there be a variety of gadgets?

Could investors be involved?

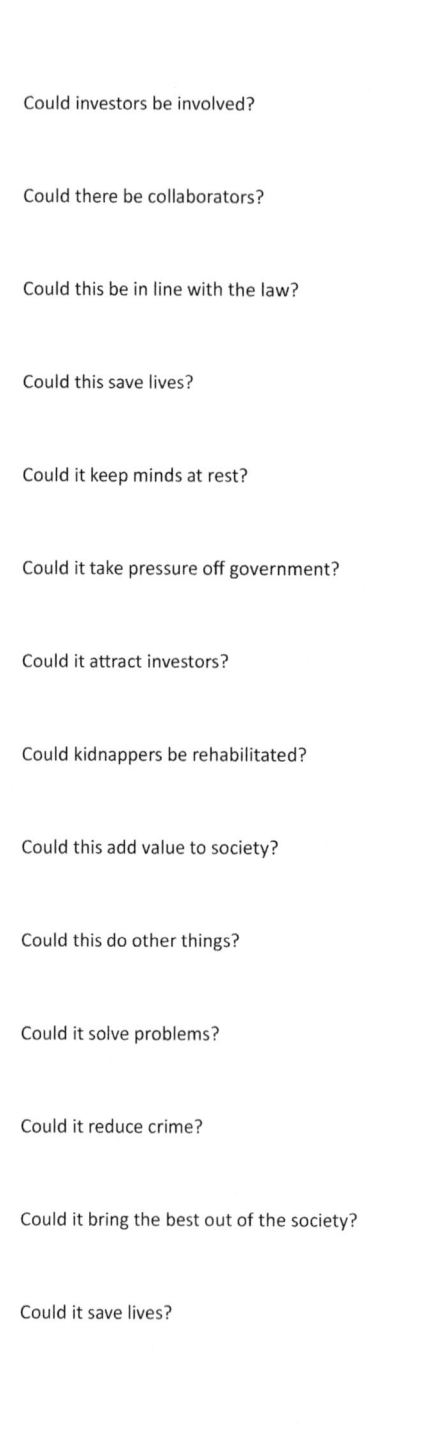

Could there be collaborators?

Could this be in line with the law?

Could this save lives?

Could it keep minds at rest?

Could it take pressure off government?

Could it attract investors?

Could kidnappers be rehabilitated?

Could this add value to society?

Could this do other things?

Could it solve problems?

Could it reduce crime?

Could it bring the best out of the society?

Could it save lives?

Could it eliminate kidnapping?

What do you think?

A Collection Of Curated Business Ideas By Jack Lookman

11. HALAL BUSINESS MICRO FINANCE

I'm a Muslim Entrepreneur

And very happy to be one

I've tasted the fruit of interest based loans

And yes, it was a lot of pain

As Muslims, we are warned

Not to partake in usury

Either as beneficiaries

Benefactors or witnesses

Those parties are cursed by Allah

And may require repentance

I remember using a great chunk of my pension

To pay off my credit card loans

After retiring from my last job

In my older years

The evil of usury dawned on me

I was lucky I had the funds

My life could have been miserable

With the possibility of suicide

The payments could quite easily

Have become unaffordable

The bailiff could have visited

Selling my belongings for little dime

Yet that may not solve the problem

I could go into more debt

And slave away just to exist

With a miserable life

After leaving the job in my mid fifties

I decided to explore my ambitions

To be an Entrepreneur…

Creating content and mentoring

To get the best of generations

To empower and impact

To add value to society

And to humanity

To attract money and wealth

To be recycled to the mission

Like they say,

Money is a a key factor in business

I searched for halal loans on the internet

For use as a small scale business

The ones I needed were hard to come by

And as usual, there are many dodgy businesses

In the market place

If I could face this problem

Others probably do

When there are problems

They present opportunities

Could there be halal financial products

For the businesses like mine?

Could high net Muslims

Put money in a pot?

Could they make profit

Without sacrificing beliefs?

Could they consider losses

As sadaqah jariyah?

Could they empower the less privileged

To attain independence?

Could they empower and inspire

From fractions of their wealth?

Could they make society richer

In ethics and values?

Could they receive barakah

From their intentions and deeds?

Does what go around

Eventually come around?

Could they sow the seeds of good

To cultivate harvests of better?

Could the thinkers and executives

Create suitable products and services?

To benefit not only Muslims

But society

Is a business opportunity created

To benefit one and all?

Or will this idea end

Once the ink goes dry?

A Collection Of Curated Business Ideas By Jack Lookman

● 12. YORUBA PROJECT

This project relates to Yoruba language

And Yoruba culture

Just as it relates to other cultures

That are streamlined

Have you noticed that some children

Don't understand the mother tongue?

Neither could they speak it

It's all about English

We sit and watch

Concerned about the rat race

Chasing money and fame

And watching the tide flow

As the children grow

Could this breed opportunity?

With the language rich...

Could we leverage technology?

To teach the language...

As well as the culture?

Could we have online schools?

And membership sites?

Could these come in text...

Audio and video?

Is the price for such

Too high to afford?

Not at all is it ...

You'll be surprised too

You could collaborate as necessary.

Where there's a will there's a way

You could add value to the children

And generations too

You could be rewarded with wealth

And recognition too

You could even become a Chief

And cultural icon

You could impact the children

And lots of generations

Giving them their identity

And enriching their lives

A word is enough for the wise

It doesn't come more than this.

A little sacrifice

For endless benefit

———————————————————————————————————

If this project interests you, please give us a shout.

Remember...

Individual hands wash each other

And both become clean.

Ire awawa ri o. (May you find the blessings that you desire)

Ire kabiti (I wish you loads of blessings)

A Collection Of Curated Business Ideas By Jack Lookman

13. FREELANCE BRAINSTORMING

You've Probably Come Across Freelance Websites

Where you could employ freelancers

This could be for the short term, or for the long term.

The process is flexible, and usually suits all parties

However, there isn't a niche for brainstormers,

Those who could assist in brainstorming

This could be in business

Or other endeavours

They could name their price

And their value proposition

This niche could be included on existing platforms

Or on stand alone platforms

As necessity demands

Some SME's could benefit from this

As a flexible resource

To brainstorm their business

From a different pair of eyes

All they need to do is visit the website

Peruse the profiles and carry out due diligence

The freelancers advertise their expertise

Their experience and exposure

A match is made and all benefit

Especially after success is achieved

In projects and money

Could you create a listing website?

Could this create jobs?

Could this create wealth?

Could people be empowered?

Could people benefit from free time?

Could this create opportunities?

Could this add value...

To individuals, and to society?

Or could it be a crazy idea...?

Awaiting space in the bin

A Collection Of Curated Business Ideas By Jack Lookman

14. BATH SPONGE

Does the bath sponge present opportunities?

When you bath and scrub...
Does your sponge wash your back effectively?
Especially the higher parts.

As an older citizen...

Can you scrub your back effectively...?
With the traditional sponge?

Do you have a positive bathing experience?

Does the soap lather well on the sponge?

Do you need to use two sponges?...

A normal one for the body...
And a long one for the back?

Is there room for improvement?

Could there be just one sponge?...
For the body and the back?

Could it create a positive user experience?

Could the sponge be of good quality?...

Collapsing and stretching as necessary?

Could the right material be used?...

By leveraging best practice?

Could it be skin-friendly...

And environmental too?

Could research be done...?

Before embarking on this project?

Is there a space in the marketplace?...

For this novel product?

Could the product be affordable

To your target demographic?

Could the price of the product...

Be competitive with its value?

Could you make lots of money

By investing in this business?

If you can't execute it alone,

Could you be part of the business chain?

Could this product benefit one…

And benefit all?

If the user experience is great?

Would the word be spread?

Could there be variants

Of the same product?

Will there be resistance

Because the idea is new?

Could this product add immense value…

Could you make lots of money?

Could it in addition…

Bring influence too?

Could you improve on the idea…

And take it to the next level?

Could this idea stimulate your thought process…

To something better?

Could you be interested in what the product is…?

I've given some clues

It's a round collapsible and extensible sponge

Which could also be stretched

For the purpose of cleaning the back

It could be stretched

It could then shrink...

To the default shape

It makes the scrubbing process

User friendly

It's two products...

For the price of one

The material of choice...

Shall be one that stretches

It should be skin sensitive...

And shall encourage soap lather

And one with a great user experience

To be worth its price

A Collection Of Curated Business Ideas By Jack Lookman

15. LEVERAGING RELIGIOUS ORGANISATIONS

Religion plays a big part in the life of Nigerians

They spend lots of time in places of worship

Sometimes, in excess of 3-4 hours weekly

As a conservative estimate

They donate part of their disposable income

Weekly or monthly to this cause

Some try to satisfy their ego

While others do it for religious or spiritual reasons

Some may even borrow

And then go into debt

Just to fulfil righteousness

For heaven they may pray

Could some of this disposable income

Be put to use for the individuals?

Could there be a cooperative…

Or other investment initiatives?

Is there any best practice

Which could be replicated?

Do the Churches and Asalatus

Have your interest at heart ?

Are they only religious organisations...

Or equally business entities?

Could you end up being well-off...

Or become very broke?

And at the peak of your poverty,

They'll concentrate on the next entity?

———————————————————————————————————

As you spend time weekly

In the place of worship

You get to know the character...

Of your brothers and sisters in faith

You get to know the trustworthy ones...

The visionaries and action takers

Could you collaborate and add value ...

To your years, young and old?

Could you carry out projects jointly...

And reap mutual benefits?

Could this be an investment for your old age?...

And part of your legacy?

Could this be a great opportunity...

To explore possibilities?

Could this be a positive consequence...

Of your religious sacrifice?

Or do you prefer to continue donating...

With the promise of heaven above?

And this heaven that is preached...

Will it be the abode of the preacher?

Could you reflect upon these words...

And take necessary action?

Could you leverage each other

Achieving the common good?

Not just making donations blindly...

For causes which you're unsure

But fulfilling your hopes and aspirations

In life and eternity

Does this give food for thought?...

Or am I a rebel without a cause?

Could you do business collaborations ...

With your fellow congregants?

Could the religious organisations ...

Have business subsidiaries?

Could the organisations empower and inspire...

With lots of common progress?

Could they proactively organise

Business courses and seminars?

Could these be digital,

To reduce cost and increase impact?

Could different members contribute from individual strengths?

Money, time or effort;

Or may be something else...

Exposure, expertise or experience?

If you are endowed with gifts...

Could you share unselfishly?

Could the more you have...

Be the more you give?

Or is it a waste of time?

With the idea dying before it's birth

A Collection Of Curated Business Ideas By Jack Lookman

16. LISTING WEBSITES FOR NIGERIANS IN DIASPORA

A listing website generally

Advertises different products and services

In most cases these are advertised at a cost

It's more like the traditional yellow pages

Except that it is digitalised

And could be niche specific

In some cases the process could be automated

Where advertisers are listed upon payment

The payment and content

Is vetted by software

In which case you could make money

While you are sleeping

You could learn how to create this

By researching the internet

Or you could get someone in IT

To help you do the needful

You could either pay for the service

Or do a collaboration

You'd profit share

And have an agreement

And carry out business processes

With due diligence

Though I've mentioned Nigerians

It could apply to other demographics

Now that you have an idea of listing websites...

You may ask how it could be applied to Nigerians in diaspora

This is a demography

Probably with similar backgrounds

They may also have

Similar interests too

They are religious, hard working

Industrious and creative

This and more

Could I have to tell

In which case...

Churches and Mosques could advertise

Business owners could.

Mentors and job adverts

And community groups too

If a new Nigerian diaspora comes to town

Your website should be one of the first go-to places

They should be able to find relatable content

Or products and services

———————————————————————————————————

In terms of monetisation

In addition to the fees for adverts

You could monetise via:

-Affiliate Marketing

-google Adsense

-Sponsors

-etc

———————————————————————————————————

I hope that you're with me

If you wish to discuss this further

Please book a 1-1 session at Jack The Mentor

Alternatively, you could research the internet

May I include a disclaimer here:

Business doesn't guarantee success

Some succeed and some fail

I'm merely presenting an idea

It's up to you to carry out your due diligence

We shall not be held liable for any failure or negativity that may come from this.

It's basically an idea which requires nurturing.

I hope that you found value

A Collection Of Curated Business Ideas By Jack Lookman

17. EMPOWERING YOUNG GRADUATES IN NIGERIA

There are unemployed people

Youths, graduates, etc

But let's focus on the graduate youths.

For them to be graduates
They probably have some desirable qualities

They may be graduates of whatever discipline.

For them to get into university
And for them to qualify

There are certain qualities that they probably have:
-research skills
-intellect
-discipline
-exposure
-etc

However, for one reason or the other
They don't have a job

They may however consider self employment

But have neither finance nor resources

They may be unable to get a mentor

One who'll smoothen the journey

At the end of the day

Some may get involved in mischief

Taking part in crime; and undesirable activities

Here comes the question:

How do you empower this demographic?

How do you monetise it?

What if you create useful content?...

For them to consume at little or no cost?

May be using free platforms like youtube or podcast

Or membership sites and blogs

Your insights may stimulate their thoughts

And guide them along the way

They may find opportunities

And leverage them

They may even volunteer with you

In exchange for this

Your content shall research useful topics

Those that resonate with them

These could be curated and edited

To suit your chosen demographic

You could even research the internet

And share useful content with them

They would already have filled a questionnaire

So that you have a feel of their pain points

You'll also get to know

Their aptitudes, and capabilities

You then find solutions

At little or no cost to them

There could be terms and conditions

For pay back or none

You could offer this service

For free or little

It could be your side hustle

Or even the main

You'd need to work out a monetisation plan

This could be via adverts or sponsorship

It could be the inclusion of premium content

It could be them exchanging service for free

They could be volunteers in what you do

Or they could be mentees with value to add

The purpose of this article is to stimulate thoughts

You could also research best practice

The core of this post,

Is to leverage the use of content

By getting the graduates

To be a part of the process

You shall leverage their intellect and expertise

In exchange for you empowering them

By showing the way processes

They could get exposed to lots of opportunities

A Collection Of Curated Business Ideas By Jack Lookman

18. X BUSINESSES YOU COULD START FOR Y THOUSAND NAIRA

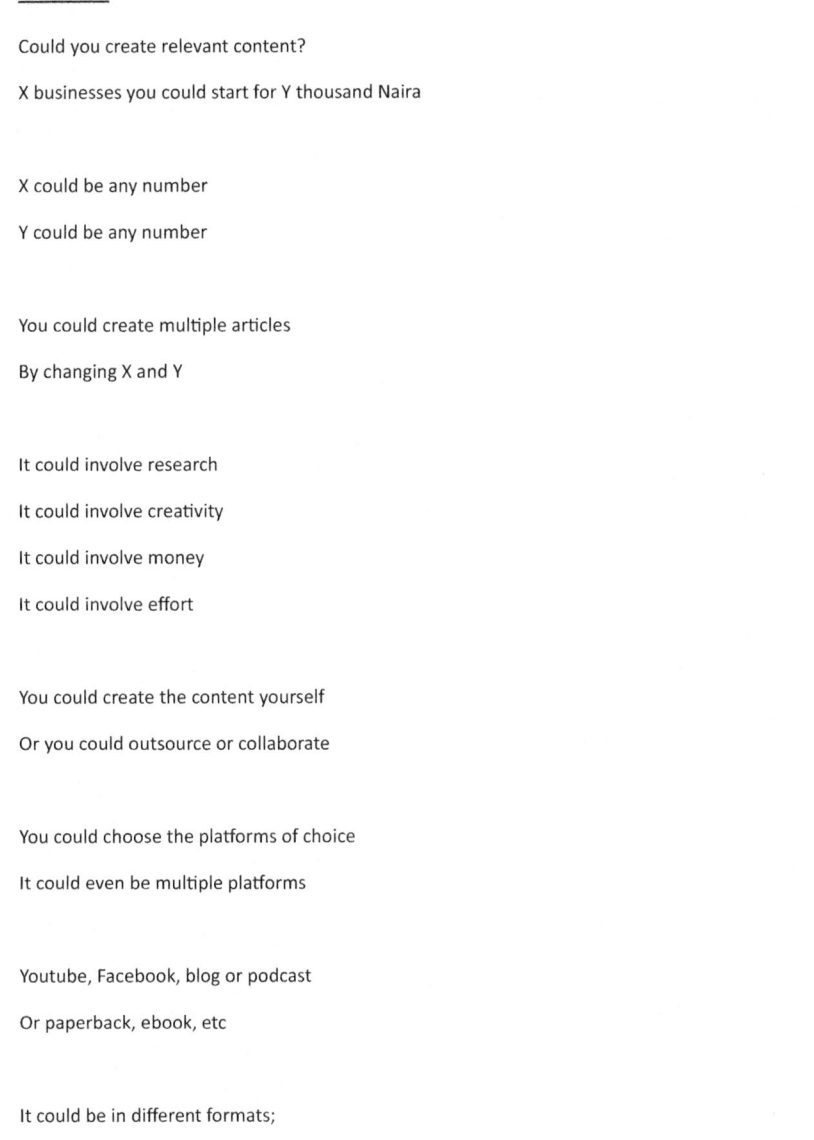

Could you create relevant content?

X businesses you could start for Y thousand Naira

X could be any number

Y could be any number

You could create multiple articles

By changing X and Y

It could involve research

It could involve creativity

It could involve money

It could involve effort

You could create the content yourself

Or you could outsource or collaborate

You could choose the platforms of choice

It could even be multiple platforms

Youtube, Facebook, blog or podcast

Or paperback, ebook, etc

It could be in different formats;

Audio, text or video

You could research monetisation models:

Adverts, affiliate marketing and sponsorships

Or public speaking, google Adsense, etc

These ideas could add value to the populace

-Job creation

-Wealth creation

-Reduced crime

-Dignity in labour

-etc

Basic resources required for this business are:

-digital device e.g. laptop, tablet, computer

-internet connection

-research skills

-collaboration skills

-interpersonal skills

-money

-etc

You could do this business on your own

Or you could collaborate with those who would compliment your resources

You need to do your research:

-market research

-competitor research

-etc

You need to carry out due diligence.

A small disclaimer is that nothing is guaranteed

People succeed and fail in business

But if you do the right things...

The chances of success are higher

If you wish to have a brainstorm with me

Please visit Jack The Mentor and book a slot

Alternatively, you could do your research

I hope that you found value

A Collection Of Curated Business Ideas By Jack Lookman

19. GROOMING VOLUNTEERS, INTERNS AND JOB SEEKERS

The work place has become extremely competitive

Even with qualifications, it's hard to get a good job

With the acquisition of skills becoming more competitive

There's the need to do something better or different

While I was growing up

I had a competitive edge

I had a tutor who helped me optimise my studies.

This concept could be applied to volunteers

Interns and job seekers

The idea, being:

-to coach the concerned persons, to have the competitive edge

-you could do this online or offline or both

-you could leverage technology

-you could collaborate with chosen others

-you could create an online platform, like a membership site or suitable other

Apart from having the relevant content

-You could streamline service users, via a questionnaire or application form

-You could create relevant content, which shall be updated as necessary

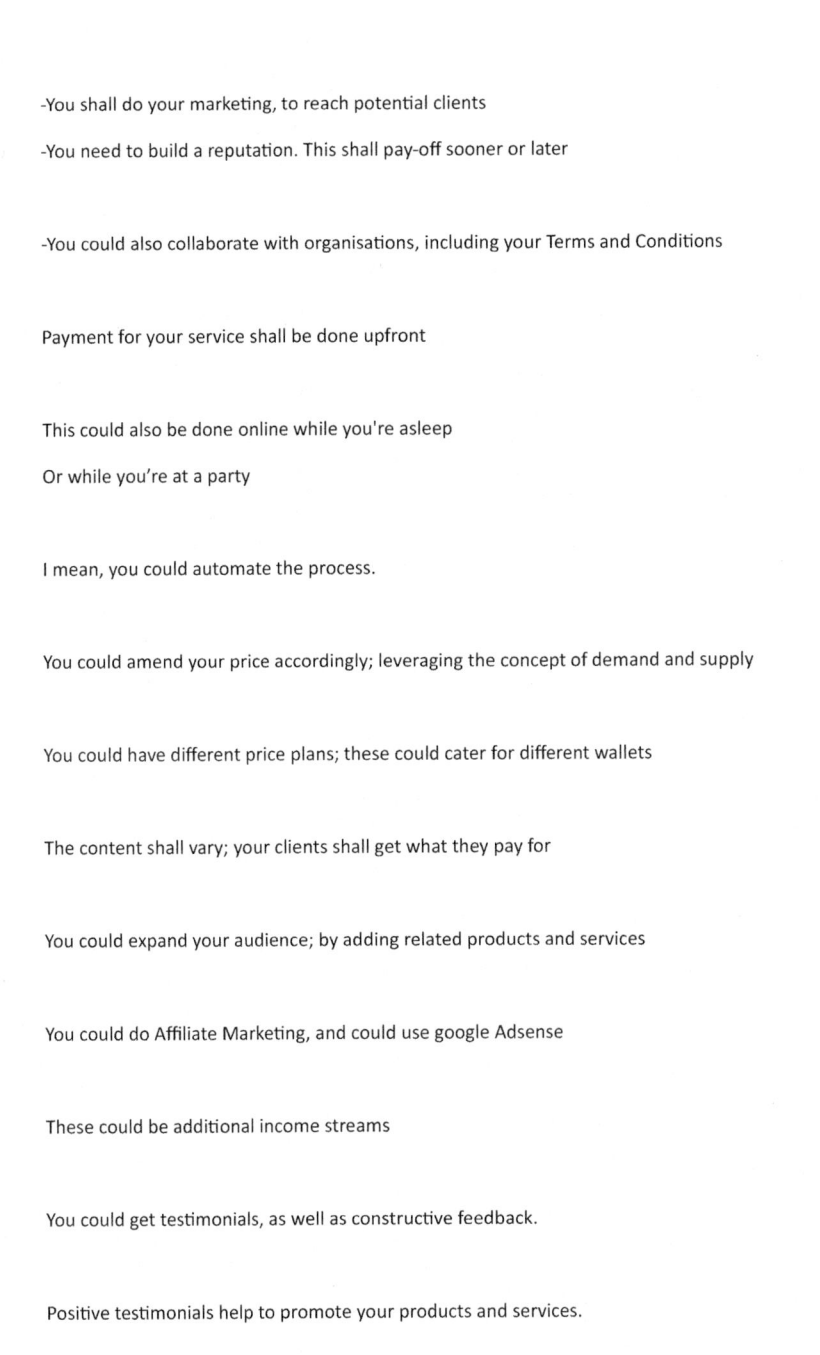

-You shall do your marketing, to reach potential clients

-You need to build a reputation. This shall pay-off sooner or later

-You could also collaborate with organisations, including your Terms and Conditions

Payment for your service shall be done upfront

This could also be done online while you're asleep

Or while you're at a party

I mean, you could automate the process.

You could amend your price accordingly; leveraging the concept of demand and supply

You could have different price plans; these could cater for different wallets

The content shall vary; your clients shall get what they pay for

You could expand your audience; by adding related products and services

You could do Affiliate Marketing, and could use google Adsense

These could be additional income streams

You could get testimonials, as well as constructive feedback.

Positive testimonials help to promote your products and services.

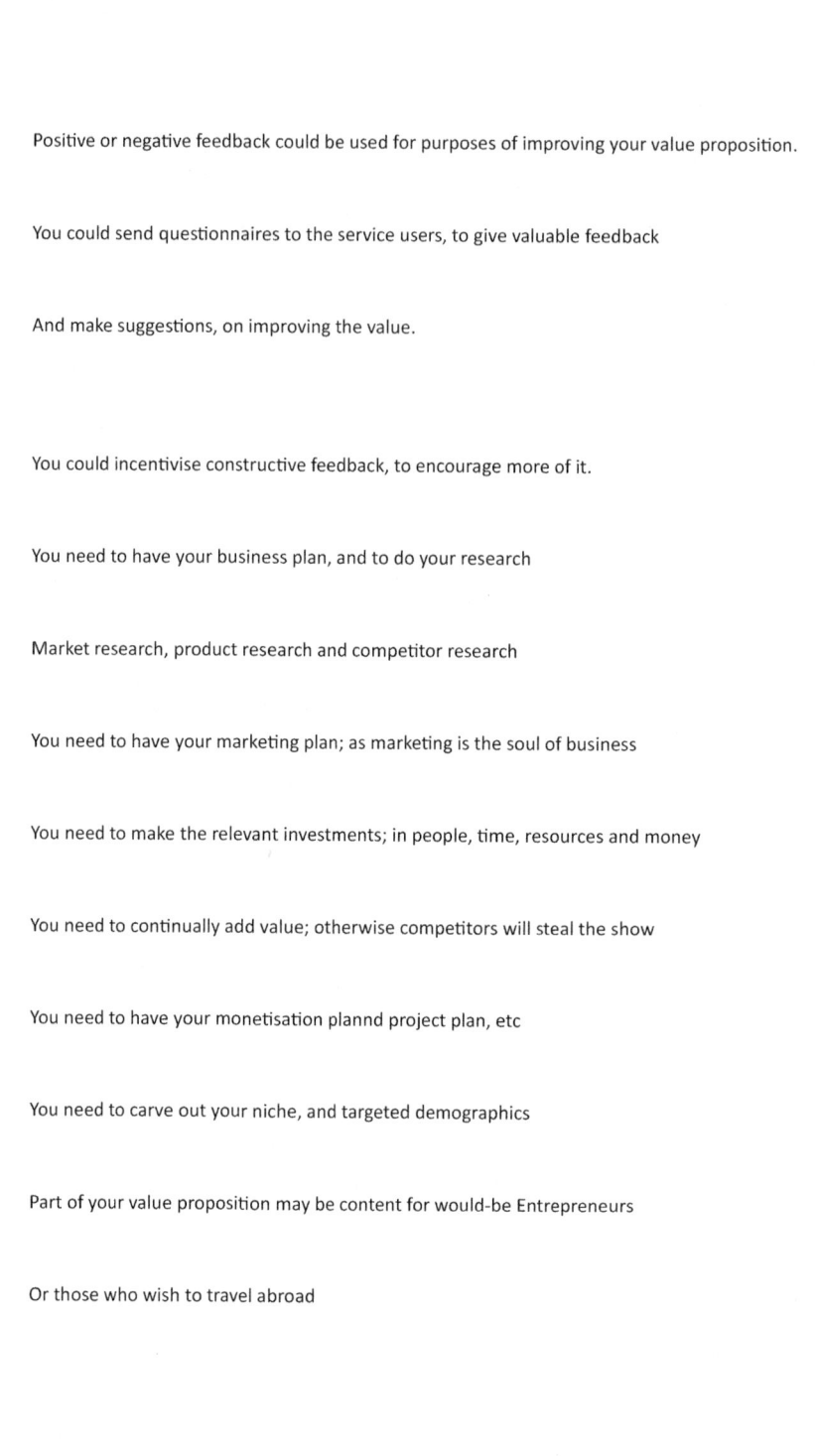

Positive or negative feedback could be used for purposes of improving your value proposition.

You could send questionnaires to the service users, to give valuable feedback

And make suggestions, on improving the value.

You could incentivise constructive feedback, to encourage more of it.

You need to have your business plan, and to do your research

Market research, product research and competitor research

You need to have your marketing plan; as marketing is the soul of business

You need to make the relevant investments; in people, time, resources and money

You need to continually add value; otherwise competitors will steal the show

You need to have your monetisation plannd project plan, etc

You need to carve out your niche, and targeted demographics

Part of your value proposition may be content for would-be Entrepreneurs

Or those who wish to travel abroad

Or opportunities, for those who seek them

You could explore your creativity

As the list could be endless

To enrich your value proposition

You could research related best practice

You could brainstorm and seek counsel

As well as carry out due diligence

Some tools required for this business are:

- a computer, laptop or tablet

- content

- online access

- a membership site

- the right mindset

- a positive attitude

- and smart effective marketing

This is a brief summary of the idea.

It's hoped that it will stimulate your creative thought process

If you wish to discuss this further

Please contact me via Jack The Mentor

Or visit our other platforms

I hope that you got value

A Collection Of Curated Business Ideas By Jack Lookman

20. MONETISING FAMILY UNIONS

Some families are deemed to be successful

While others are not

Failed marital unions

Could happen to anyone

It may not be a personality issue

But may be one of compatibility

It may even be caused

Due to external factors

Or factors beyond control

Whatever side

Of the coin that it may be

It presents an entrepreneurial opportunity

For all to see

Most people want to have

Successful happy families

A home they look forward to

Retiring to a conducive environment

One in which they all thrive

One that helps build a great society

You may ask what the business opportunity is

This, I shall tell

You could create content

In different formats and on different platforms

It may be in different languages

For different demographics

For the beautiful families,

They could share best practice

Their successes, their challenges, their failures, etc

You could create a questionnaire

And follow up with audio interaction

It's better for them to be anonymous

To maintain confidentiality

You'd probably get more information

Out of them that way

If they wish to be compensated

That could be arranged

And could be included in your budget

To manage any costs

As for the failed family unions

You want to find out what went wrong

What pitfalls to be avoided

What they could do differently

The same process as before could be applied

You could collate a data base of the different experiences

You could articulate it into fictional content

You could present it to your audience

And then monetise

Suggested platforms are:

Ebooks, blog, paperback and podcast

You could also use social media, etc

What benefits could be derived?

So may you ask

It could help to positively engineer society

The divorce rate could be reduced

The younger and older ones could learn real life lessons

It could create jobs and opportunities

It could create wealth

It could add value to society

It could bring about a happier and healthier society

This list could be long

The target audience are youths, parents and guardians

Professional marriage counsellors, religious clerics, etc

To monetise the products

You could sell the books

You could have a subscription or membership website

You could monetise via youtube, facebook and social media

You could monetise your blog via adverts and sponsorships,

Affiliate marketing, google Adsense, etc

The idea is raw and may require perfection

These are my little thoughts to ponder

As I pull the curtain

A Collection Of Curated Business Ideas By Jack Lookman

ABOUT THE AUTHOR

Olayinka Carew, aka Jack Lookman is the 1st of 5 Children.

He has 3 children, and elderly mum. He is resident in the United Kingdom and is of Nigerian origin.

This is his 15th book.

He studied at King's College, Lagos and University of Lagos.

He has varied life and work experiences.

He has been involved in voluntary and paid jobs.

He is dedicating the rest of his life to empowering and inspiring generations.

This is one of his legacy projects.

Though he has health challenges, he does not let that halt his mission and vision.

Even though he studied Engineering at University; his calling is so many miles away from that. He is currently a Content Creator, Affiliate Marketer, Entrepreneur and Mentor.

He is the Director and Owner of Jack Lookman Limited, a registered business in the United Kingdom and their aim is to empower and inspire generations by leveraging the internet.

OTHER BOOKS BY THE AUTHOR

1. Despair, Submission, Faith & Hope – Volume 1
2. Despair, Submission, Faith & Hope – Volume 2
3. Monetising Digital Book Reviews
4. E-Commerce For Traditional African Attires
5. Basic Management And Fundraising Tip For Community Groups
6. Monetising A Digital Library
7. Ajo, The App And Opportunities
8. Empowering Orphans, Widows and Widowers
9. Submission, Gratitude, Faith and Hope
10. Oro Ishiti- Indelible Yoruba Words
11. Eid Monetisation by Leveraging Technology
12. Jaaloo Puzzles- Volume 1
13. Jaaloo Puzzles- Volume 2
14. What are your thoughts? What is your mindset?

FOR MORE RESOURCES FROM JACK LOOKMAN LIMITED, USE THE LINKS BELOW

Olayinka Carew aka Jack Lookman

Jack's Empowerment: https://www.jacksempowerment.com

Jaaloo Puzzles: https://www.jaaloo.com

Jack Lookman: https://jacklookman.co.uk

Amazon books: https://amzn.to/3jahxEC   (or search for Jack Lookman at amazon.com or amazon.co.uk)

Become a member of Jack Lookman's Facebook Community: https://www.facebook.com/jack.lookman.3 (or search for Jack Lookman on Facebook)

Facebook Page: Jack's Favourite Poems: https://www.facebook.com/jacksfavouritepoems

As well as at : Opo Ati Orukan: https://bit.ly/OpoAtiOrukan

And Facebook group: Business Ideas etc: https://bit.ly/BusinessIdeasetc

Subscribe to Jack Lookman's Youtube Channel: https://youtube.com/@jacklookman (or search for Jack Lookman)

Connect on LinkedIn: Olayinka Carew aka Jack Lookman

Email: jacklookman@yahoo.co.uk

At Jack Lookman Limited there are opportunities for investors and collaborators.

Ire o (I wish you blessings)

Ire kabiti (I wish you loads of blessings)

Printed in Great Britain
by Amazon